BLACK BOYS DESERVE FLOWERS TOO

BY BRIANNA LAREN

Printed in the United States of America

ISBN: 978-8-218-29253-9
(Paperback)
ISBN: 979-8-890-90356-3
(E-Book)

SCAN QR CODE TO ACCESS THE LEARNING GUIDE FOR THIS BOOK

This book is dedicated to

Bam & Bella
Zaire Burroughs
Jarryl Jefferson Jr
Earl "EJ" Powell
Atakan R. Brown
Deacon Hawk
TJ Statham
Xavier
PJ & Zion
Na'Sim

Carter James
Dominic Tyler
Nick, Joey, & Mikey
Drew, Kyler, & Kaleb
Kavyn & Brody
David Benoit II
Jude Richardson
Johnathan
EJ Stokes
Ezrah

**To the first man I ever loved & who ever loved me, My Daddy
and to the Black Men who played a role in my life & deserve flowers too**

Kem W. Taylor
Kellen Taylor
DaVonn Pyatt
Lawrence Taylor
Clarence Taylor Jr.
TJ Taylor
Valdis Terrell
Clarence Taylor
Anthony Minor
Arthur Polite
Melvin Zanders
Otis Simpson
Darren Avery
Franklin Winters
Marcus Gladden

Theron Thomas
Russell Johnson
Miguel Sanchez
Rashad Mooreman
Jahmeal Quarles-Belt
Bishop Bryan Pierce
Jeremy Graham
Jerel Brown
Will Taylor
Doug Brown
Coach Rags
Jonathan Foote
Paul Graves
Jerome Freeland
Malcolm Bryant
Billy Edringston

In Loving Memory of

Alston Kirkland Jr
Bill & Brent Dorsey
Garland Watson
Shannon Canon

DID YOU KNOW YOU DESERVE
FLOWERS TOO? WELL YOU DO.

FLOWERS, LOVE, AND APPRECIATION
JUST FOR BEING YOU

YOU DESERVE APPLAUSE, CHEERS, & PRAISE.

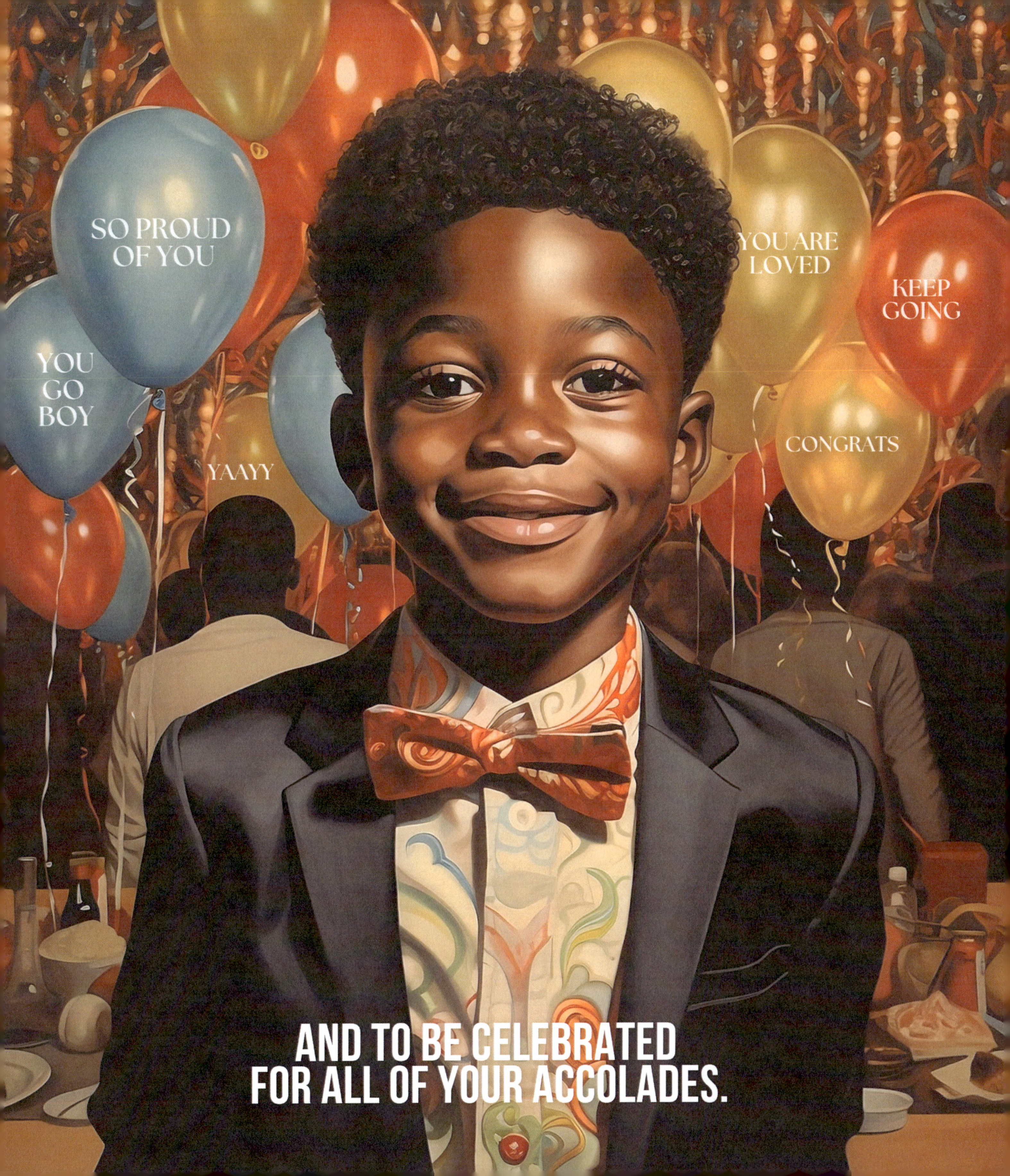
SO PROUD OF YOU
YOU ARE LOVED
KEEP GOING
YOU GO BOY
CONGRATS
YAAYY
AND TO BE CELEBRATED
FOR ALL OF YOUR ACCOLADES.

YOU DESERVE TO EXPLORE THE WORLD
WITHOUT LIMITS AND WITHOUT FEAR.

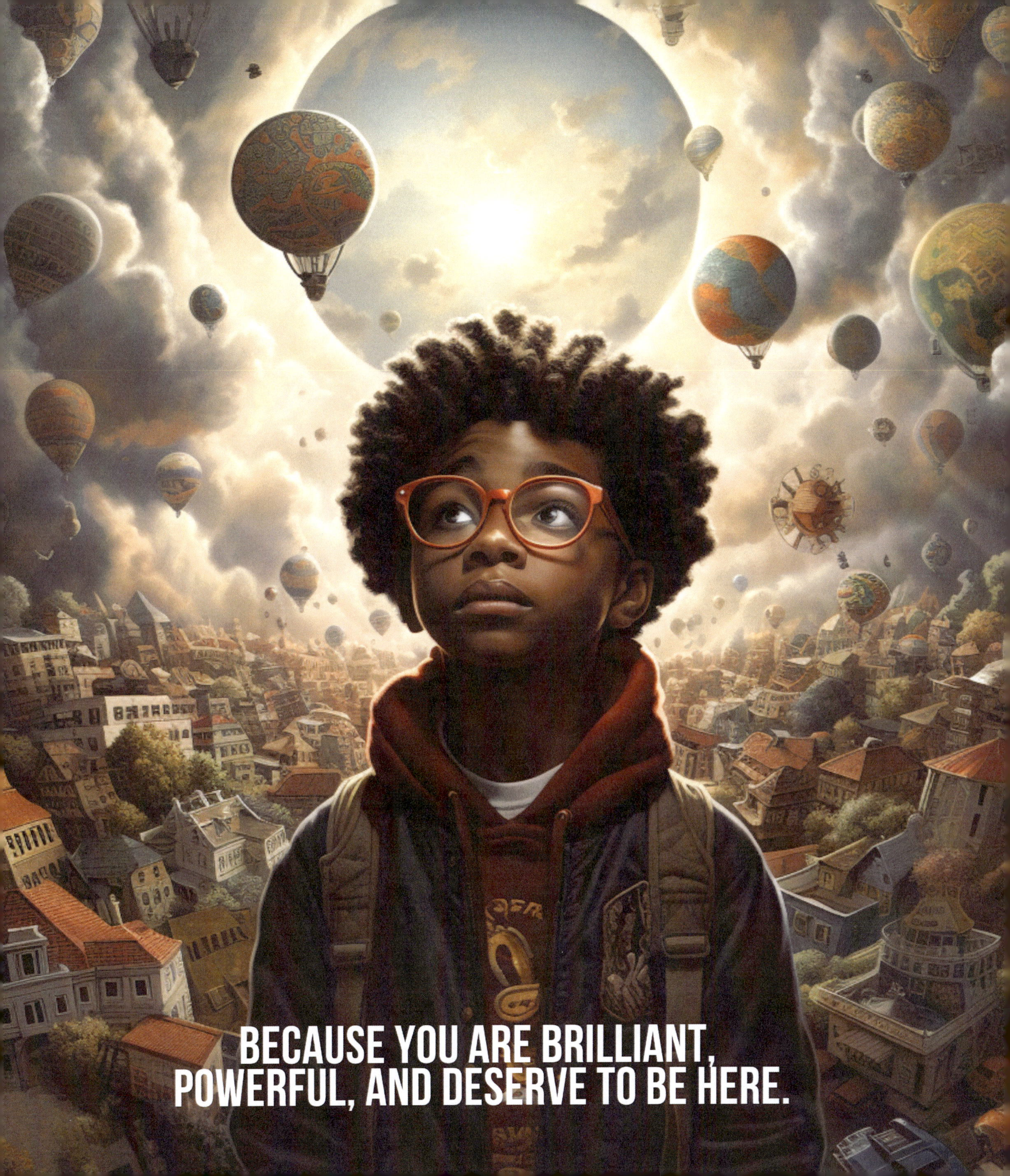
BECAUSE YOU ARE BRILLIANT,
POWERFUL, AND DESERVE TO BE HERE.

YOU DESERVE TO LEARN THAT YOU ARE NOT ONLY
DESCENDANTS OF PEOPLE THAT WERE ENSLAVED.

THOSE WHO CAME BEFORE YOU WERE ALSO
DETERMINED, INTELLIGENT, AND BRAVE.

YOU DESERVE TO EXPERIENCE JOY, PEACE, LAUGHTER AND EVERYTHING IN BETWEEN.

AND TO ALWAYS FEEL HEARD,
VALUED, AND SEEN

YOU DESERVE TO FEEL AT HOME.

AND TO KNOW THAT YOU ARE NEVER TRULY ALONE.

YOU DESERVE TO DREAM BIG DREAMS
AND LET YOUR IMAGINATION RUN WILD.

AND ENJOY THE FREEDOM OF BEING A CHILD.

YOU DESERVE THE CHANCE TO
MAKE THOSE BIG DREAMS REAL.

AND THE SPACE TO GROW,
THRIVE, AND HEAL.

YOU DESERVE TO BE SNUGGLED
AND CUDDLED, YES YOU DO.

KNOW THAT IT IS OKAY TO FEEL YOUR
FEELINGS BECAUSE BOYS AND MEN CRY TOO.

YOU DESERVE TO GROW OLD

AND LEAVE NO
STORY UNTOLD

BUT JUST BECAUSE YOU DESERVE SOMETHING
DOES NOT MEAN YOU WILL GET IT.

THAT IS WHY IT IS SO IMPORTANT TO
KNOW WHO YOU ARE AND STAND IN IT.

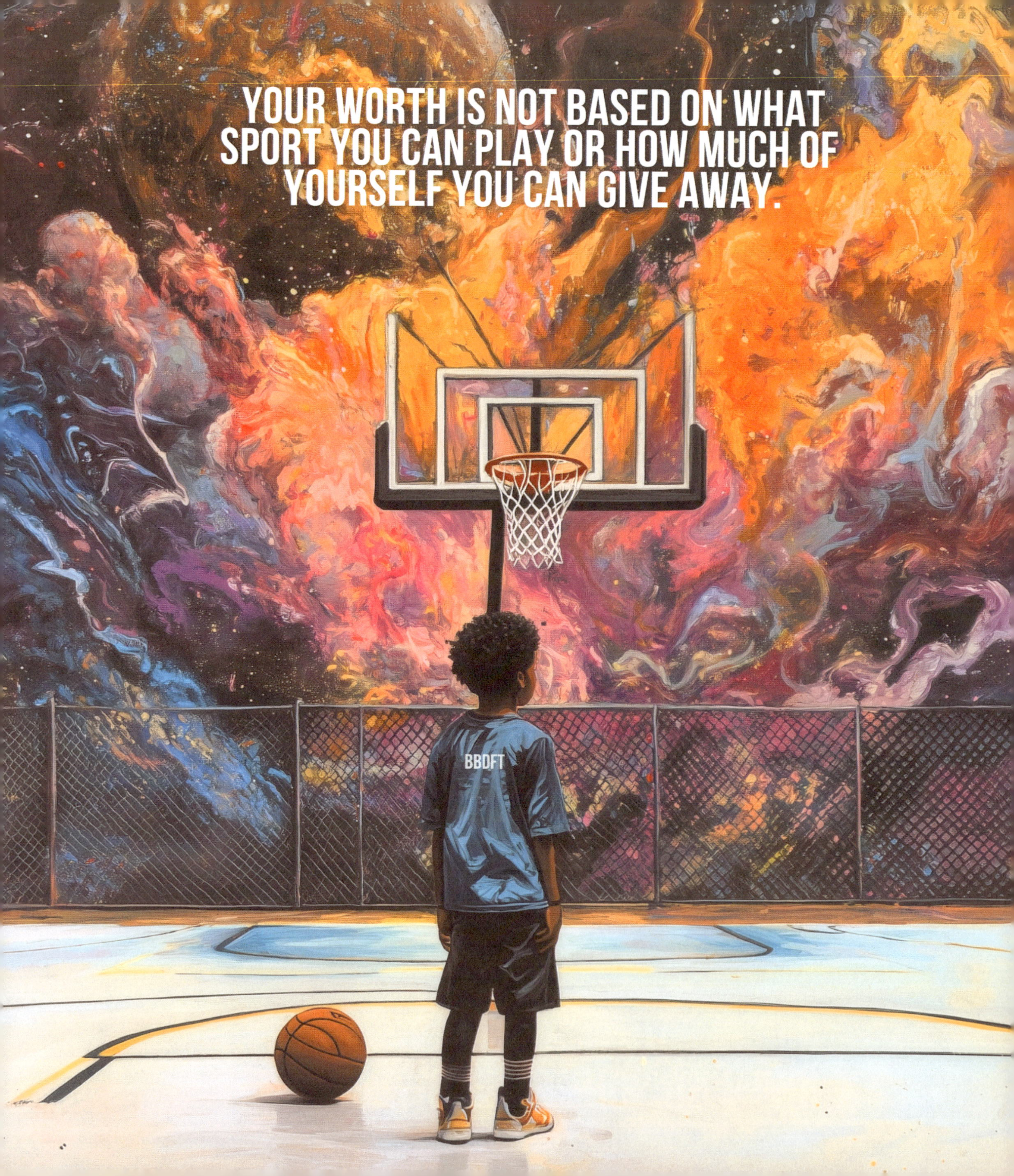

YOUR WORTH IS NOT BASED ON WHAT SPORT YOU CAN PLAY OR HOW MUCH OF YOURSELF YOU CAN GIVE AWAY.
BBDFT

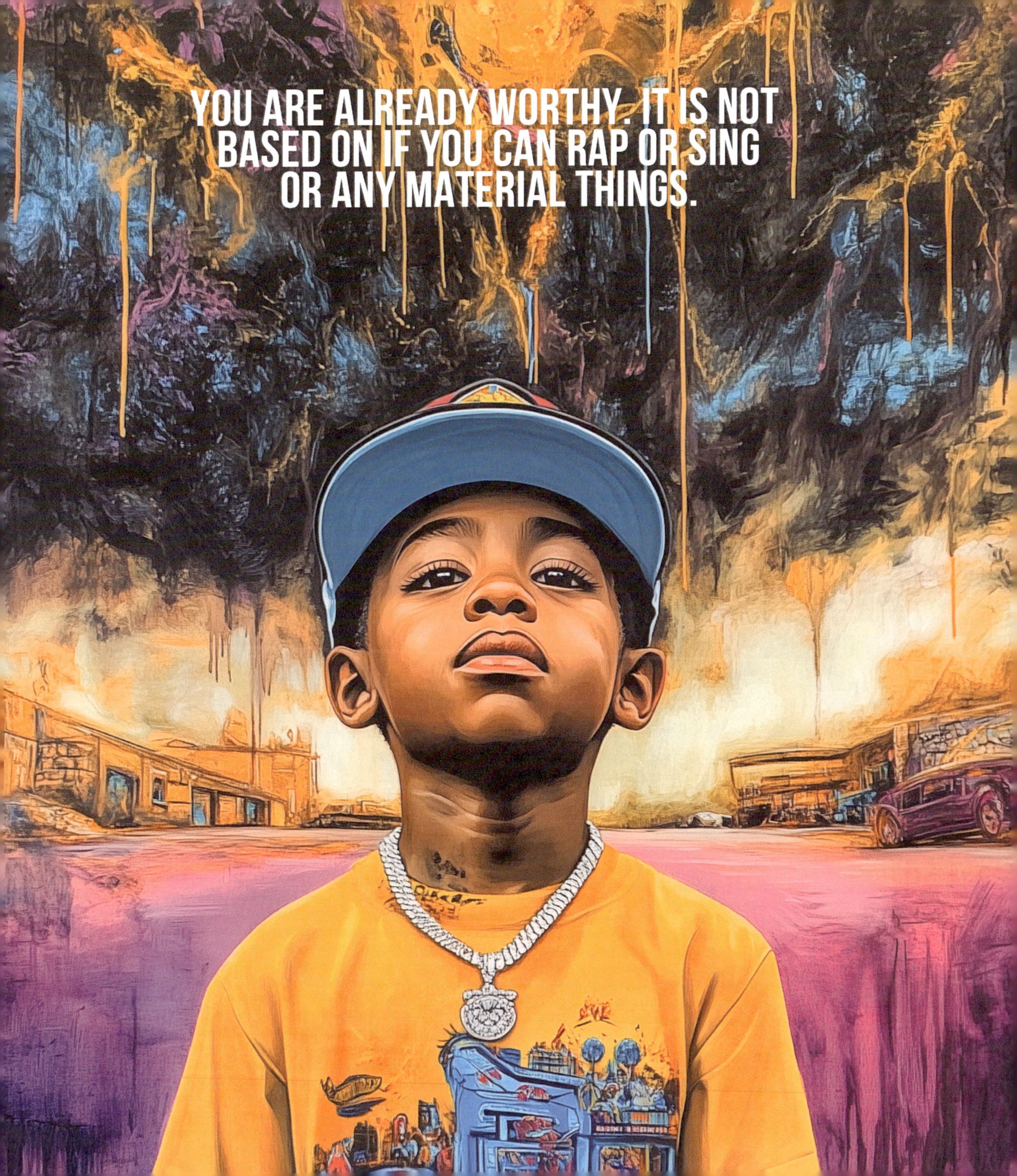

YOU ARE ALREADY WORTHY. IT IS NOT
BASED ON IF YOU CAN RAP OR SING
OR ANY MATERIAL THINGS.

THE WORLD WILL TRY TO CONVINCE
YOU OF THINGS THAT ARE UNTRUE.

SO YOU MUST BE BOLD AND
CONFIDENT IN ALL THAT YOU DO.

PEOPLE WILL NOT ALWAYS SEE YOUR
VALUE, SO YOU HAVE TO SEE IT.

THEY MAY NOT KNOW WHAT YOU ARE CAPABLE OF,
SO YOU WILL HAVE TO BELIEVE IT.

IT WON'T BE EASY AND YOU MAY
SINK BEFORE YOU SWIM.

BUT NO MATTER WHAT, NO ONE CAN STEAL YOUR JOY OR STRENGTH, BECAUSE THOSE COME FROM WITHIN.

IF YOU DID NOT KNOW BEFORE,
I HOPE NOW YOU DO.

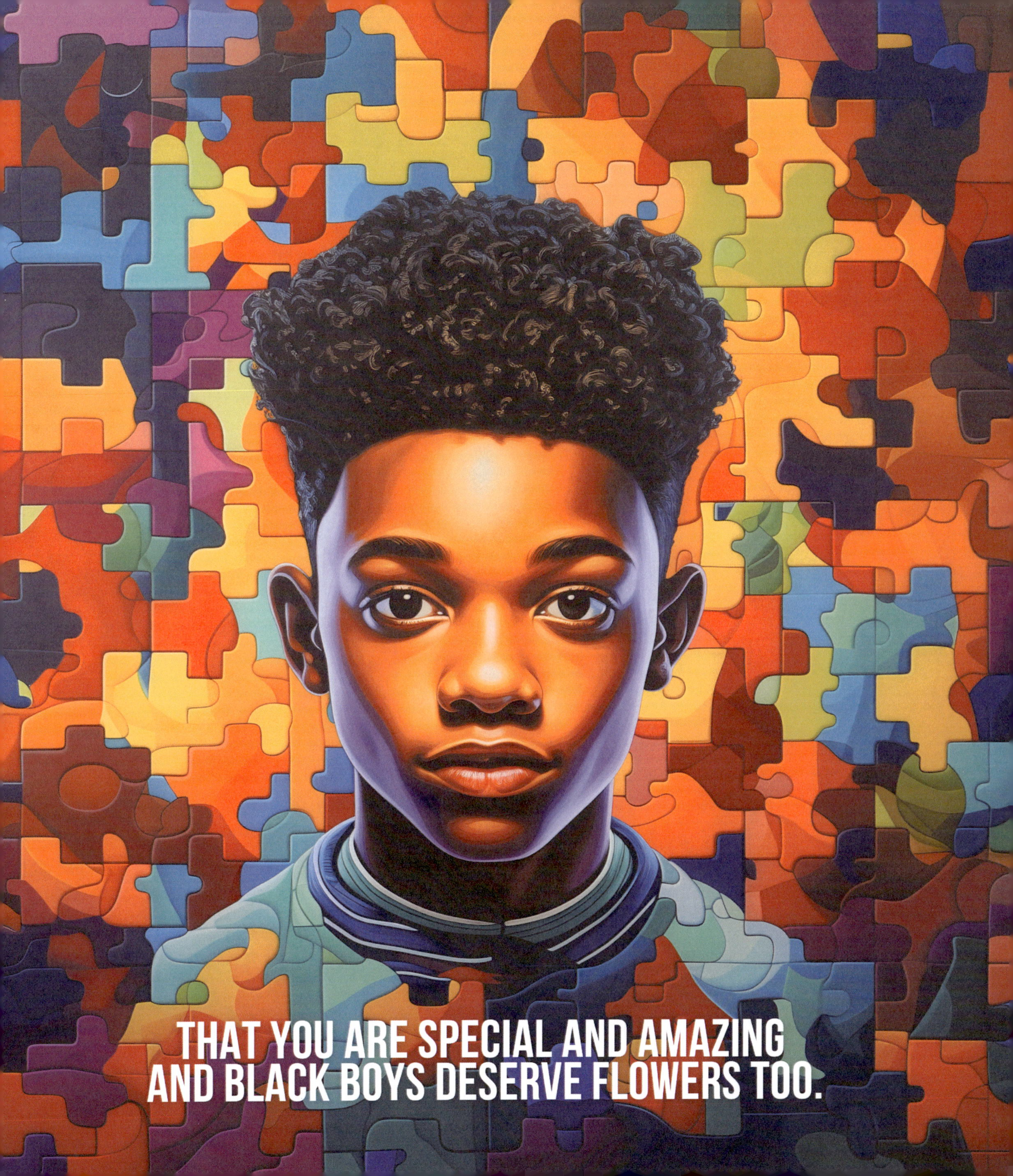

THAT YOU ARE SPECIAL AND AMAZING
AND BLACK BOYS DESERVE FLOWERS TOO.

ABOUT THE AUTHOR

Brianna Laren is an author who not only creates stories but also transforms lives. Her journey is one of purpose and her brand is synonymous with empowerment, resilience, and the celebration of Black excellence. With each page turned in her books, readers embark on a journey of self-discovery and affirmation, finding strength and beauty in their own stories.

Brianna has penned Breebe's Brand New Baby Brother, Pretty Pretty Black Girl, Edge Control for the Soul, Save Your Edges Workbook, Pretty Pretty Black Girl: The Children's Book, Black Boys Deserve Flowers Too, and Black Boys Deserve to Thrive Too Workbook.

www.BriannaLaren.com
Photo Credit: Jodie Brim